CUENTO
DE LUZ

This collection of children's books, inspired by real stories, comes from the heart, and as a result of a collaboration between the What Really Matters Foundation, and the publisher Cuento de Luz.

We share the same dreams, the same hopes, and the same philosophy about spreading universal values.

We hope that families, schools, libraries, adults and children all around the world enjoy these books; that they are both inspired and moved by them, and discover, if they do not know it already, what really matters.

María Franco
What Really Matters Foundation
www.loquedeverdadimporta.org

Ana Eulate
Cuento de Luz
www.cuentodeluz.com

Rafa Nadal
Text © 2016 Marta Barroso
Illustrations © 2016 Monica Carretero
This edition © 2016 Cuento de Luz SL
Calle Claveles, 10 | Urb. Monteclaro | Pozuelo de Alarcón | 28223 | Madrid | Spain
www.cuentodeluz.com
Title in Spanish: Rafa Nadal
English translation by Jon Brokenbrow
ISBN: 978-84-16733-07-1
Printed in PRC by Shanghai Chenxi Printing Co., Ltd. August 2016, print number 1589-6

STONE
PAPER

NO TREES · NO WATER · NO BLEACH

RAFA NADAL

"What really matters is being happy along the way, not waiting until you reach the **finish** line."

Rafa Nadal

Marta Barroso

Illustrated by **Mónica Carretero**

A little boy sat down on a park bench. Hope was sitting there too.

"Who are you?" he asked.

"I am Hope," she said.

"What's that? I've never heard of hope before."

"Well, maybe you're just too little to understand," she said. The little boy took a deep breath, and asked her again. "But what is it?" he said, bursting to know the answer.

Hope smiled at him, and tried to explain. "It's that feeling you get when you really, really want something to happen."

"Lots of grown-ups think I'm something that's hard to achieve, but I swear to you that if you believe in yourself, if you think positively and you work hard to make your dream come true, then I'll be there for you. Hope is the joy of living."

The little boy looked at her with a doubtful expression. But his inquisitive nature led him to ask another question. "Do you think you could explain all that with an example? I think I'm going to really like what you're trying to say." Hope thought for a moment, and set to work. She looked for all the right words, and put them all in the right place, and decided to use them to tell a story; a story that the little boy could keep in his heart, and which would help him to grow. She closed her eyes, and began.

Once upon a time, there was a little boy who loved tennis and soccer, just like so many other children in every corner of the world. His name was Rafael, and he was four years old. He spent the whole day kicking a ball around, and glued to a tennis racket.

Sometimes he dreamed about being a professional soccer player, just like his Uncle Toni. He had told Rafa that he had been one of the stars of the soccer team AC Milan, and had been known all over the world as "The Great Natali," thanks to his amazing skills with the ball.

Uncle Toni would tell Rafa all about the most incredible moments of his career, especially the brilliant goal he'd scored that won his team the European Cup, thanks to a fantastic pass from his teammate Spaghetti.

"Or was it Macaroni? Never mind!" said his uncle, his memory clouded by so much emotion. All of his teammates were equally important to him, and he knew that he would never have been so famous without them. Rafa, innocently, agreed with him.

Rafa ran off to tell his parents, Sebastian and Ana Maria, together with his sister, Maribel, all about the fabulous feats of the Great Natali. They all smiled at him lovingly as he talked about his uncle's amazing career. His father shook his head from side to side and laughed about the stories his brother Toni had made up.

Rafa's life was very much like that of any other little boy. He was very good, and quite shy, and was lucky enough to have a family that was very close. Every weekend, they would meet up with all of his uncles and cousins at their grandparents' house, and they would have wonderful meals together, where they would chat, share their ideas, and listen to what everyone had to say. "I'm so lucky!" Rafa often thought to himself.

Rafa's uncle may not have really been a soccer star, but he did know everything there was to know about tennis. Uncle Toni taught him to play at tennis lessons with other children, and Rafa really began to shine at the sport. That is when tennis balls started to take the place of his soccer ball.

The Great Natali knew straight away that his nephew had a special talent for playing tennis. He began to train him even harder, telling him over and over again that the most important thing of all was to be enthusiastic about what he did. "Rafael, if you are keen about playing and you enjoy what you do, then everything else will just fall right into place, on and off the tennis court." Rafa understood what he meant, because hope and enthusiasm had always formed a part of his life in one way or another.

It turned out that his Uncle Toni was also a magician, with a special passion about everything he did. He believed in it so much that he was even able to make Rafa become invisible, in front of the whole family. They all gasped in amazement as he disappeared before their eyes, and the glass he was holding in his hand wobbled around the room. They couldn't stop laughing! Another time, Toni transferred his incredible powers through the TV screen to help a tennis player win, when his opponent was behaving very rudely.

As a result, Rafa learned from a very early age the importance of the word *respect*, and promised his uncle that he would always try to enter the court with a smile on his face. And so, almost without realizing it, he gradually learned all about values. And he learned how to win, and he learned how to lose.

When Rafa was only eight years old, he had to stand in for an injured player from the older children's team who were all over the age of twelve. There was nobody else who could play in his place, and as they were traveling toward the tournament, his uncle and trainer turned to him and said, "Don't worry about a thing. You'll probably lose, but keep fighting right through to the end. And if I see that you're having a bad time, I'll make it rain, and the match will be cancelled." Rafa looked at him in amazement, and because he believed in him with all of his heart, he knew that he would be able to do it.

True enough, Rafa started to lose. 1-0, 2-0, 3-0, 4-0, 5-0. During the rest period, he ran toward his uncle, and sat down on the bench. Toni said to him: "Enjoy yourself, and keep fighting right through to the end."

Rafa walked back onto the court with his uncle's words ringing in his ears, and began to win. When the score had reached 5-4, it began to rain, and they stopped the match. He looked at his uncle, walked up to him quietly, and whispered: "Natali, can you stop the rain? I think I can win." But Toni, the Great Natali, the wizard, preferred to leave things just the way they were.

"I don't know if it's because he couldn't, or if it's because he decided that Rafa had to learn to lose," said Hope, thoughtfully, "but the rain stopped anyhow, and Rafa didn't win the match. It's just as important to know how to lose as it is to know how to win."

Rafa continued to win, and by the age of 11 he was a Spanish champion, winning tournaments in all categories. Perhaps the most important was when he won the international Les Petits As tournament.

It was the start of a truly outstanding career; the first steps that defined a personality marked by sincerity, humility, respect, gratefulness and responsibility.

"You will only learn that every action has an effect if you take responsibility for your acts," Toni would tell him. "If you want to be number one, then you must be responsible, and don't forget that this requires great effort. But not only in tennis, Rafael. In everything you do in your life."

"Whether you're a teacher, a writer or a cook, they all have to behave with the responsibility that comes with trying to be the best. And don't forget something very, very important. Being number one in the profession you've chosen in life means only that. In the rest of your daily life you're just the same as everyone else." And so, always at each other's side, they began to fill their world with hope.

Rafa grew older and kept training, every day, under the watchful eye of his Uncle Toni, who always treated him as if he were his own son, while still respecting the important role of Rafa's mother and father. He trained him hard, preparing him for his adult life and as a professional tennis player, always reminding him: "Everything you learn at professional level will affect the way you live."

Little by little, step by step, working on his mind and his body, Rafa became the world's number one tennis player, and an example for millions of people.

He was an idol for children and adults alike. Rafael became Rafa for his countless fans, and in the good times and the bad times, his personality never changed. He worked hard, without ever complaining, without ever changing the way he was.

He learned what his uncle had taught him over and over again: to make tennis a simple sport.

Rafa appreciated the importance of the people around him: his team, which had been by his side throughout his entire career. The team always joined his family in the box reserved for them at all of the international tournaments.

That is where Rafa would look for support when things got tough. And he was always grateful for everything that was happening to him. "I'm so lucky!" he would say, over and over again.

"I ran after my dream, and I caught up with it. I've worked on it, and I'm still living it. It's been hard work, but it's been worth the effort. I'm really happy, and all I can say is thank you."

A smile spread across the little boy's face. "I don't think it's that easy!" he thought. But Hope, who was there, deep inside him, heard his thoughts as clear as day. "No, if it were easy, it wouldn't mean a thing. You can't become successful just by having special qualities. More than anything, it's about hard work, organization, effort, and determination. You have to fight for what you want, and along the way, to discover *what really matters*. My presence helps people make their dreams a reality, by always looking at the positive side of things."

Many years later, the little boy who was listening to Hope grew up to be a man, and told the same story to his son, this time from his own perspective. Through his example, Rafa taught him to fight for his dreams. And through his words, Toni helped him to get ahead and to discover the positive side of life: the joy of living.

About the *What Really Matters Foundation*

The aim of the What Really Matters Foundation is to promote universal values in society. Its main project consists of the What Really Matters conferences, which are aimed at young people.

Every year, they are held in eight cities in Spain, and in another six countries. During the conferences, a series of speakers share the real and inspiring stories of their lives, which invite us to discover the things that are really important in life. Like the story in the book you're holding in your hands.

You can join us, hear more stories, and find out a little more about us at www.loquedeverdadimporta.org.

We look forward to your visit!

María Franco
What Really Matters Foundation